THE SONG OF SONGS

BORGO PRESS BOOKS BY S. FOWLER WRIGHT

Arresting Delia: An Inspector Cleveland Classic Crime Novel
The Attic Murder: An Inspector Combridge & Mr. Jellipot Classic Crime Novel
The Bell Street Murders: An Inspector Combridge & Mr. Jellipot Classic Crime Novel
Beyond the Rim: A Lost Race Fantasy
Black Widow: A Classic Crime Novel
The British Colonies: No Surrender to Nazi Germany!
The Capone Caper: Mr. Jellipot vs. the King of Crime: A Classic Crime Novel
Crime & Co.: An Inspector Cleveland Classic Crime Novel
Dawn: A Novel of Global Warming
Dead by Saturday: An Inspector Cleveland Classic Crime Novel
Dream; or, The Simian Maid: A Fantasy of Prehistory (Marguerite Cranleigh #1)
Elfwin: An Historical Novel of Anglo-Saxon Times
The End of the Mildew Gang: An Inspector Cauldron Classic Crime Novel (Mildew Gang #3)
Four Callers in Razor Street: An Inspector Combridge & Mr. Jellipot Classic Crime Novel
Four Days' War: The Alternate World War II, Book Two
The Hanging of Constance Hillier: An Inspector Cleveland Classic Crime Novel
The Hidden Tribe: A Lost Race Fantasy
The Jordans Murder: An Inspector Combridge & Mr. Jellipot Classic Crime Novel
The King Against Anne Bickerton: A Classic Crime Novel
Megiddo's Ridge: The Alternate World War II, Book Three
The Mildew Gang: An Inspector Cauldron Classic Crime Novel (Mildew Gang #1)
Murder in Bethnal Square: An Inspector Combridge & Mr. Jellipot Classic Crime Novel
The Police and the Public: Some Thoughts on the British System of Justice
Post-Mortem Evidence: An Inspector Combridge & Mr. Jellipot Classic Crime Novel
Prelude in Prague: The Alternate World War II, Book One
The Return of the Mildew Gang: An Inspector Cauldron Classic Crime Novel (Mildew Gang #2)
The Rissole Mystery: An Inspector Combridge & Mr. Jellipot Classic Crime Novel
The Screaming Lake: A Lost Race Fantasy
The Secret of the Screen: An Inspector Combridge & Mr. Jellipot Classic Crime Novel
The Song of Songs and Other Poems
Spiders' War: A Novel of the Far Future (Marguerite Cranleigh #3)
Three Witnesses: A Classic Crime Novel
Too Much for Mr. Jellipot: An Inspector Combridge & Mr. Jellipot Classic Crime Novel
The Vengeance of Gwa: A Fantasy of Prehistory (Marguerite Cranleigh #2)
Was Murder Done? A Classic Crime Novel
Who Murdered Reynard? A Classic Crime Novel
The Wills of Jane Kanwhistle: An Inspector Combridge & Mr. Jellipot Classic Crime Novel
With Cause Enough?: An Inspector Combridge & Mr. Jellipot Classic Crime Novel

THE SONG OF SONGS

AND OTHER POEMS

by

S. FOWLER WRIGHT

THE BORGO PRESS

An Imprint of Wildside Press LLC

MMIX

Copyright © 1925, 1929, 1958 by S. Fowler Wright
Copyright © 2009 by the Estate of S. Fowler Wright

All rights reserved.
No part of this book may be reproduced in any form
without the expressed written consent
of the author and publisher.

www.wildsidepress.com

FIRST WILDSIDE EDITION

CONTENTS

About the Author 6
Preface 7
Compiler's Note 15

The Song of Songs 17

Scene 1—Outside the Palace of Solomon 18
Scene 2—At the Gate of Jerusalem 25
Scene 3—The Judgement Seat of Solomon 29
Scene 4—In the Palace of Solomon 34
Scene 5—The Vineyards of Baal-Hamon 42

Some Songs of Bilitis 51
Songs of Balochistan 73

ABOUT THE AUTHOR

SYDNEY FOWLER WRIGHT (1874-1965) penned over seventy volumes of science fiction, fantasy, classic mysteries, historical novels, poetry, and non-fiction, many of them being published by the Borgo Press Imprint of Wildside Press. Please visit his website at:

www.sfw.org

PREFACE

THE first poem in this book, "The Song of Songs," originally appeared in *Poetry* (February, 1925), and the first edition of the present volume was issued in the autumn of the same year.

In preparing a second edition, I think it may be advantageous to reproduce an explanatory note on the poem that appeared in the above-mentioned issue of *Poetry*.

"Having expressed the opinion," I wrote, "that the free verse of the Authorised Version is unapproachably excellent, it may seem surprising that I should have attempted a rendering of the 'Song of Songs' in a regular stanzaic form. My aim has been not to offer an alternative translation, but to reconstruct a poem, the original of which exists only in disordered and inconsequent fragments; and, in doing this, I have preferred a form of verse that I am least incompetent to handle.

"The difficulties of interpretation are very great, under any of the conflicting theories that have been advanced by successive commentators. The mystical or allegorical theory, which held the field for many centuries, has few advocates today. Its weakness lies in the fact that it is entirely arbitrary, being unsupported by any internal evidence; and, in any case, it is unsatisfactory, because it does nothing to elucidate the narrative itself, and even an allegory must be understood before its mystical meaning can be pursued to any likely capture.

"The more popular modern view presents it as a moral tale, in which a virtuous maiden of northern Palestine resists the allurements of Solomon's harem, in fervour of a shepherd, to whom she is finally restored by the magnanimity of the king.

"There is nothing inherently impossible, or even absurd, in this theory, if we remove the modern garb in which it is presented, and realise that, though the young lady might have acted in this manner (human nature being unchangeable), it would not have been any more 'virtuous,' in view of the national customs of her time, than had she preferred to join the royal establishment.

"The theory postulates a moral convention which was simply not there, or, at most, it was the propriety of Solomon's conduct in unusual circumstances, and not that of the Shulamite, which would have been placed in the balance.

"The authorship is too doubtful for any argument to be based upon it, and it is not impossible, though it may seem unlikely, that Solomon himself should have written a poem with such a theme; but, whether this interpretation be plausible or not, it is certain that it has gained advocacy through the desire of the theologians to introduce what they suppose to be a moral value into a poem of an obviously erotic kind.

"If we put this bias aside, and examine it with an open mind, we find, under this interpretation, that which was previously disorder increased to chaos.

"Briefly, I regard the following propositions as defensible:

1. That the poem has reached us only in an incomplete form, and that the parts of what remains are probably disordered.

2. That, even in its present form, the evidences of its original structure are sufficient to show that it was dramatic rather than lyric, being in the same tradition as the later Hellenic dramas of the fifth century B.C., the main action taking place off the stage in the same way, and being in the mouths of the chorus, though the choral elaborations of strophe, antistrophe, and epode may not have been within the conception of the Hebrew poet.
3. That the main outlines of the plot are these: Solomon, visiting his vineyards at Baal-Hamon, makes the acquaintance, and wins the love, of a Shulamite girl who is employed there, and leaves her without disclosing his identity. She follows him to Jerusalem, where a dream that he is at her door causes her to walk out in her sleep to find him when she is arrested by the night-watch, but subsequently released. Afterwards, recognising the King, she boldly—and successfully—claims that he should acknowledge the bond between them. In the last scene, they have returned to Baal-Hamon together, where the Shulamite realises and laments the precarious nature of her

hold upon Solomon, in contrast to the confidence she had felt at their first meeting, and is reassured by Solomon and the Chorus, so far as reassurance is possible.

"However early difficulties may be surmounted, I do not see how the final chapter can be made to support any other interpretation.

"The passionate and despairing cry with which it opens:

'O that thou wert as my brother—!'

simply has no meaning, if we suppose her to be restored to a lover of her own rank, and the development of the argument is incomprehensible.

"Finally, I have made it a primary aim, as I always do in work of this kind, to maintain the integrity of the author's conception, so far as I am able to understand it. In this endeavour, and in reshaping a broken thing, I found it necessary first to write a long poem and then to reduce it to a very moderate compass.

"I have possibly used the pruning-knife with too great a severity. I am conscious of having sacrificed some stanzas that may be individually better than others that have survived them, but it has appeared to me to be a primary consideration to maintain the unity and the simplicity of the original poem, with the fewest possible additions of extraneous matter.

"In one or two details in which I have deviated from the accepted translations, as in reversing the implication of Chapter II, v. 17—

> ...not yet the shadows close,
> Not yet the night is nigh,

I am supported both by modern scholarship and by literary probability. In others, such as the reference to the 'little sister,' which seems to be impossible of any certain decision, I have at least suggested a plausible sequence of argument on the part of the Chorus—that it is better to have taken the adventure of love, with all its dangers, 'than never to have loved at all,' instead of the orthodox explanation of the commentators, which is both inconsequent and unconvincing; and the response of the Shulamite supports my interpretation.

"Still, this is merely guessing a way out of an obscurity, and I am probably mistaken.

"The most frequent, and, at first sight, the strongest objection to this construction is that the book would never have found a place in the sacred canon of Hebrew writings if it had not been regarded as having some 'moral' significance, such as is supposed to lie in the loyalty of the Shulamite to a poor and distant lover. I reply that such a theme would have had no moral significance, whatever its romantic attraction might have been, and I suggest that the book was not included in the Hebrew canon till its original meaning had been lost, after more than one century of precarious wandering and mutilation, and when its actual significance may have been almost as conjectural as it is today. Further, the Hebrew canon accepted the tale of Esther, in which no human ingenuity could discover any religious or ethical altitude, incidentally demonstrating that historical novels were written somewhat earlier than the eighteenth century."

The second section of the book, the 'Songs of Bilitis', owes obvious acknowledgement to Pierre

Louys; and the 'Songs of Balochistan' to originals collected orally, and transcribed by Longworth Dames in the later part of the nineteenth century.

—S. Fowler Wright

COMPILER'S NOTE

This poem almost certainly was written with S.F.W.'s first wife, Nellie (d. 1918), in mind. The 1958 'Mcfarlane Speech' refers:

> Is ashes all the verse I made,
>   The verse for only you.
> Retrieveless, save the years return,
>   The years that proved it true.
>
> More deep the living sights we saw
>   The dying days conceal,
> —(Our Warwicks on the Flanders plain,
>   Zouaves at Abbeville)—

More dark around the land you loved
    The clouds of winter close:
Amid surrendered seas we steer
    To rocks that no man knows.

I see not from what separate ways
    In other dawn we meet,
Nor how shall He Whose thought we are
    His broken tale complete,

But spring has found your daffodils
    With gallant hearts and high
That like in your birth-month are born,
    And like in April die,

And till this dark earth's mystery
    Its hidden end fulfils
The ring is on your hand—and on
    Your heart the daffodils.

March 1925

THE SONG OF SONGS

Characters:

Solomon
The Shulamite
Chorus of the Daughters of Jerusalem

>Heed not behind, beyond, the while ye kiss
>   On throat, and lips, and eyes.
>Be nought the primal void, the last abyss,
>   Where the spent darkness lies.

SCENE ONE

OUTSIDE THE PALACE OF SOLOMON

SHULAMITE:

> O that the kisses of his mouth again
> > My lips might taste and live!
> Were here delight, though here delight
> > was slain,
> > More than the grape could give.

CHORUS:

> Who art thou that the watchmen found
> > by night
> > In darkened streets astray?
> Are hundreds gathered for their lord's
> > delight,
> > But fairer thou than they.
>
> We saw thee fairer in their place than
> > all

> That grace the great king's train,
> Behind whose feet the harem's curtains fall,
> Or Kedar's tents contain.

SHULAMITE:

> Behold, O daughters of Jerusalem,
> From cedared hills I come,
> Dove-haunted, that, to hear the voice of them,
> The summer winds are dumb.
>
> I take no shame for aught that once hath been,
> I take no shame that now
> Above the fairness of my breasts is seen
> Darkness of throat and brow.
>
> In the long vales beneath El Hamon lie
> The vineyards of the king.
> There would I watch the waiting hours go by
> From dawn to evening.

When sleeping silent in the noonday
   glare
   The stilled zenanas lay,
I wandered on the sun-loved slopes to
   scare
   The seeking fox away.

I kept full harvest on the planted lands
   For the king's slaves to reap.
The full grape-clusters hung for
   gleaning hands,
   —But mine I did not keep.

A shepherd from the further hills he
   came.
   No nearer name I knew.
Love to swift love outleaped so clear a
   flame
   That shame and fear it slew.

CHORUS:

O fairest of all daughters born of men,
   If nothing more he told,
Return, and seek from sheltered glen to

    glen,
        From builded fold to fold.

    The footsteps of the feeding flocks
        behind
        Were better path to try.
    Here where ye seek your shepherd love
        to find
        The city streets deny.

SHULAMITE:

    I seek him here, for well my heart
        replied
        That city streets he trod.
    No shepherd he, that down the
        mountain side
        Strayed like a lonely god.

    He called me through the dreams the
        darkness bears:
        The pleading voice I knew:
    I heard his steps upon the outer stairs:
        His hair was dank with dew.

While calling in the outer dark he stands,
  Shall I not meet his prayer?
I felt along the night with empty hands,
  And there was no man there.

The watchmen found me where I walked astray,
  The keepers of the gate.
They seized me there as one that brawls—as they
  The night's importunate.

CHORUS:

They fared as those on whom the sunlight shines,
  From darkened rooms who tread.
They found thee fairer than the concubines
  Far lands have tributed.

SHULAMITE:

I felt rude hands upon my shoulders lie,

I heard rude voices call,
Aware of night-wind, and the open sky,
Of moonlight on the wall,

Of shadowed houses on the long street-
 side,
Of bare and bleeding feet,
Was here no dream, but all my grief I
 cried
Along the startled street.

CHORUS:

They seized thee rudely as a thing
 unclean,
But when thy veil was rent
Was no such star their humbled eyes
 had seen
In all love's firmament.

They brought thee to the palace doors at
 last,
In the king's ward to bide.
The queens upon thy face their glances
 cast:

The eunuchs spake aside.

They bid thee seek him whom thy soul
    allied
In thy familiar north.
The queens in haste thy present needs
    supplied:
The eunuchs thrust thee forth.

SCENE TWO

AT THE GATE OF JERUSALEM

CHORUS:

> Far down from where the coastward mountains bend
> The Sheban queen hath gone.
> Her camels from Beth-Horon's pass descend
> The Vale of Ajalon.

SHULAMITE:

> Who comes in purple from the wilderness?
> The city gates are wide.
> Four after four, to break the thronging press,
> The serried horsemen ride.

CHORUS:

>Behold, he enters from a queen's farewell,
>>Great David's heir is he.
>His right hand reaches to Palmyra's well,
>>His left to Egypt's sea.

>Lord is he of strange lands Arabian,
>>Of desert routes away,
>Of Red Sea fleets that lean Sidonians man,
>>Of cargoes of Cathay.

>He takes the tributes of a hundred kings,
>>Gold and chalcedony,
>With all the powders that the merchant brings,
>>And apes and ivory.

SHULAMITE:

>I see, three-score, Benaiah's ranks

>   advance,
>   The guard of Israel's lord.
> Gleams down the file Judea's shortened
>   lance:
>   Gleams the Assyrian sword.

CHORUS:

>   On chariot-housings, fold on Tyrian
>   fold,
>   The dazzling sunlight smites;
>   On weaponed guards agleam with
>   Ophir's gold;
>   And brass-greaved Pelethites.
>
>   He cometh midmost of his glorious
>   train,
>   The wide land's lord is he.
>   His chariot's purples are an army slain:
>   Its stems are ivory:
>
>   Great Zion's virgins pave its floor with
>   love:
>   Its panelled sides are bright
>   With silvered cedar, and with gold

above,
For all his ways are light.

SHULAMITE:

Behold, my lover and my prince is mine:
My shepherd-king is one.
Well spake, from those dove-haunted rocks of thine,
Ye winds of Lebanon!

SCENE THREE

THE JUDGEMENT SEAT OF SOLOMON

CHORUS:

>Who dares to thrust her nobler lords aside
>>Along the rising hall?
>Who fails unmeet her waiting place to bide
>>At this high festival?

SHULAMITE:

>Why should I leave for aught my taken mate,
>>With other flocks to stray?
>I seek him whom my soul desires, so late
>>Between my breasts who lay.

>For lo! no more the winter rains were

blind,
The winter dark was done.
I looked from out my lattice screen to find
The over-mounting sun.

Again in all the winds his voice I heard,
The winds afore that sighed
Through the high pillars, where the mating bird
Moaned in our House of Pride.

Again as in the summer grass we lay,
The cedars branched above,
The pines' great rafters stretched their curtains grey,
That roofed our House of Love.

As once I led thee to Amana's height,
On Hermon's mountains wide,
Where roared the lions through the frighted night,
And Senir's caves replied—

As once we dared the triple peaks of

>   snow,
>   The leopard-dens we found,
>   The forests dwindled in the vales
>   below,
>   The eagles screamed around—
>
>   Shall I not dare thee in thy seated state?
>   Shalt thou not own my plea?
>   What though thy captains close with
>   swords await?
>   For what are these to thee?

CHORUS:

>   He looketh from his lioned throne and
>   high;
>   The crown Bath-sheba placed
>   On brows made glad for Egypt's
>   nuptials nigh
>   His royal state hath graced.

SOLOMON:

>   Among the maidens of thy land thou art
>   The lily's crimson ray,

That through the choking brambles
breaks apart:
The piercing thorns are they.

SHULAMITE:

Thou art the tree that all the noonday
heat
Shades from me where I lie,
The while I reach its pleasant fruits to
eat.
The sheltered flower am I.

SOLOMON:

Thou art the iris of the watered plain.
The weary days are gone.
Thou bringest to my longing thought
again
The scent of Lebanon.

CHORUS:

Behold, he brings her to his banquet
hall,
To the High Seat. Above

The haughtier blazons of the trophied wall
The banner hangs of Love.

SCENE FOUR

IN THE PALACE OF SOLOMON

CHORUS:

> Return, return, thy peasant dress forget,
>   Return, O Shulamite!
> Then shall we see as whom from Gilead met
>   The shining Sons of Light.

SOLOMON:

> I heard the queens, among themselves
>   who spake,
>   "Behold, the moon is bare;
> The blue night pauses, lest a cloud
>   should flake
>   A visioned sight so fair."
>
> I heard the virgins of Jerusalem,
>   Among themselves who said,

"Behold, she is the dawn on Bethlehem,
   When the cold night is fled."

I heard the voices of the concubines,
   When that clear sun they saw,
"Behold, the lighting of her eyes
      outshines
   The thousand blades of war."

CHORUS:

The night is breathless where she
      comes. The day
   Of all her light is full.
She is two armies in their joined array,
   And both invincible.

SOLOMON:

She cometh as a dove from distant
      heights,
   From cliffs inviolate,
Where the moon wanders in the lonely
      nights
   On hills inanimate.

CHORUS:

> O prince's daughter! how thy beauties
>   rise,
>   From small feet silken-shod:
> The pillared smoothness of thy perfect
>   thighs
>   Shaped by an Egean god.
>
> Thy belly is a rounded goblet filled
>   With love's delighting wine;
> A threshold where the ready wheat is
>   hilled;
>   A lily-fragranced shrine.
>
> As two young roes thy level breasts are
>   twin;
>   Thy neck an ivory tower;
> Thine eyes are pools, with shadowed
>   lights therein,
>   When falls the twilight hour,
>
> Are pools of Heshbon which the
>   darkness hoods,

> Bath-Rabbim's gate below:
> Thine head is Carmel, clothed in purple
> woods,
> Before the month of snow.
>
> Thy stature is a palm in shadeless sand,
> Stately, and straight, and tall.
> Thy breasts are grapes that wait the
> gleaner's hand:
> There is no grape shall fall.

SOLOMON:

> Thou art a garden where no eyes
> intrude,
> A garden walled; and I,
> As wide above thy terraced pools doth
> brood
> The overclosing sky.

CHORUS:

> Thou art a garden for thy chosen king,
> High-walled and gated thus.
> Planted with choice of every scented

        thing,
And fruits delicious.

SHULAMITE:

> To him be nought denied, and nought be hid,
> Thicket and vale, and hill;
> But he shall walk their pleasant paths amid,
> Rejoicing where he will.

SOLOMON:

> There in the place of grapes and garnage fair
> I tread my paths alone.
> Shall no man reach its ripened fruits and rare,
> Shall no man share my throne.

SHULAMITE:

> O north wind, rise! O pleasant south, awake!

And on my garden blow,
That from stooped boughs the ready
fruit he break;
And all its odours know.

CHORUS:

Treads the young roe adown the
flowery way,
The snowy heights behind,
Where lurks the doe that loves the
shaded day,
Her darkened couch to find.

SHULAMITE:

Be here thy coming as the eager roe,
Down scented ways to tread,
Between the lifted hills of warmer snow
To find thy fragrant bed.

CHORUS:

More than the pride his kingly fate
fulfils

> Is his desire to her.
> The lifted sweetness of her breasts is
>   hills
> Of frankincense and myrrh.

SHULAMITE:

> Therefore is his right arm about me
>   cast,
> His left beneath my head,
> Finding its night, though longéd night
>   be past,
> Where the loosed hair is shed

CHORUS:

> O hands, O lips, that conquer where
>   they will,
> And where they conquer kiss!
> Love leaps awake that so should life
>   fulfil
> No lesser end than this.

SHULAMITE:

> O love, lie still! Not yet the shadows close,
> Not yet the night is nigh;
> Behold, thou treadest as the feeding roes
> On Bethur's mountains high.

SCENE FIVE

THE VINEYARDS OF BAAL-HAMON

SHULAMITE:

>Oh, let us with the longer days return
>   To that north land we knew,
>When first we joined the lores of love
>   to learn;
>   Where the green vineyards grew.

CHORUS:

>Who is it to her mother's place returned
>   On her belov'd who leans,
>Who once unveiled the summer suns
>   had burned,
>   Preferred to Israel's queens?

SHULAMITE:

>Oh, come we where the chestnut's

>   leaves expand,
>   For summer wins the year.
>   The vines are green along the singing land,
>   The tender buds appear.
>
>   Alone once more in springing vales to stray;
>   In village walls to dwell;
>   Far from the splendours of thy courts away,
>   Our dearer loves to tell.
>
>   The cedars walled us, and the mighty pines
>   Their rafters closed above;
>   No trophy of thy meaner halls outshines
>   Our banner there of Love.

SOLOMON:

>   Once more beneath Amana's heights of snow
>   Faint with great love to lie.
>   Thou wert the verdure of the vale

below:
The feeding hart was I.

SHULAMITE:

Oh, that thou wert as one like-born to me,
  To peasant breasts that clung,
Joined the same toils in simple lives as we,
  And spake the mountain tongue!

Then wert thou at my mother's feet preferred,
  Our common loves to bless;
Nor other voice against its peace were heard
  Deflower love's wilderness.

Not then should wisdom call thine heart away,
  Nor foolish cares should rise,
Nor envy speak what love had shamed to say,
  Nor Egypt's queen despise.

I have no Gezer for thy gift. I lack
    Barbarian gauds to bring.
Spice-laden fleets the south winds bear
    thee back
    I cannot yield my king.

Oh, seal me to thee, compassed heart
    and arm,
    With stronger love than death,
That jealous hate may find no place to
    harm
    With its dividing breath!

CHORUS:

    The grave is cruel, and its grasp is cold,
        But here is darker death.
    It seizeth with a most vehement hold,
        That all love sundereth.

SOLOMON:

    There is no price the merchant's scales
        can tell

That shall Love's purchase pay.
All that man hath, to reach His mart,
were well
Cast and contemned away.

CHORUS:

There is no wealth that furthest orient
flings
Before the great king's feet,
No glory of supernal fire that springs
Where night and morning meet,

But dulls to earth, or doth its wings
retreat
In Love's full dawn—a God
Beneath the coming of Whose
shining feet
The morning stars are trod.

SOLOMON:

There are no powers shall cast Love's
empire down,
There are no floods shall chill,

>   Earth hath not seas His chosen paths to
>   drown,
>   Who walketh where He will.

CHORUS:

>   There are no fires but here their force
>   were vain;
>   There are no floods shall drown;
>   There are no gods that earth's last ends
>   contain
>   Powerful to cast Him down.

SHULAMITE:

>   Where Baal-Hamon meets the morning
>   light
>   The royal vineyards lay.
>   I wandered on the sun-loved slopes to
>   fright
>   The thieving fox away.
>
>   I am the vineyard of my chosen king,
>   His pleasant fruits to bear.
>   What pits hath Love, what nets shall
>   Wisdom bring,

The cunning fox to snare?

CHORUS:

We have a sister, and she hath no
  breasts,
 She hath no breasts to give,
Where love might rest, when love from
  longing rests,
 Or feeding life might live.

A little sister, and she hath no breasts,
 Her hands, her lips, are cold.
Shall she have any comfort where she
  rests
 For cedar walls or gold?

SHULAMITE:

But I am like a garnished hold and tall,
 My breasts are towers that stand
The outer corners of the fortressed wall,
 Lords of a conquered land.

Heed not behind, beyond, the while ye

>   kiss
>   On throat, and lips, and eyes.
>   Be naught the primal void, the last
>   abyss,
>   Where the spent darkness lies.

SOME SONGS OF BILITIS

I.
MY FATHER WAS A WANDERING GREEK

    My father was a wandering Greek. A fair
        Phoenician girl he saw,
    Woo'd, and begot, and left who would not share
        His tribe's Odysseyan law.

    Pamphylia saw my birth. My venturous feet
        Its wildest mountains trod.
    I watched them from my bolder search retreat—
        Satyr, and nymph, and god.

The sources of the world were mine,
> beside
>> Its secret streams. The same
Where Paris woo'd, and where Œnone
> died,
>> And Aphrodite came.

And though close death my nearer sight
> may blind,
>> Mine eyes' last light shall know
The great gloom of the mighty woods
> behind,
>> The shining seas below.

II.

MY HAIR WAS BLOWN ACROSS MY MOUTH

My hair was blown across my mouth.
> My feet
>> Sank in the mountain snow.
He said, *What think ye in these wilds to
> meet,
>> That in such haste ye go?*

There was a satyr in the vale, I said;
  I traced it where it trod.
He said, The satyrs with the fauns are dead;
  Nor oread lives, nor god.

But rest thou by the fire I make, and I
  A naiad's tomb will show.
With iron-shod staff he smote the stream-bed dry,
  And told the tomb below.

He said, *The winter binds the hills more fast*
  Than ten years' space should know.
He bore me lamb-like o'er his shoulder cast
  Down the long slopes of snow.

III.
FROM WHEN THE NIGHT INVADES THE WOODLAND SKY

From when the night invades the woodland sky,

Beneath the branches low,
The world is ours, its secret haunts to
 try,
Its nameless ways to go.

The wild cat, hunting, heeds not where
 we tread;
Shades of the night are we.
The wild deer, hearing, lifts a startled
 head,
And turns mild eyes to see.

The stars can light not here, too faint
 and few,
Through cypress, larch and fir.
The thickets where we break are
 drenched with dew,
And when the night winds stir,

A meaning to the wakened sense is
 brought,
Surer than sound or sight—
Diviner is not than the scent unthought
 Of roses in the night.

IV.
It Is Not for the Shrine of Artemis

It is not for the shrine of Artemis,
    Where those of Perga pray,
Though is not known a milder rule than
    this,
    And wise of heart are they.

It is not for Athene's awful brows,
    Though wharves of Sidon see
The wealth her grace her hardy sect
    allows,
    Piled gold and ivory.

It is for one that in my heart is throned,
    I twist the iris sweet,
Whose heart as mine its tender need
    hath owned—
    For Aphrodite's feet.

I will not speak aloud the thing I would,
    But I will whisper low,
Faint-heard as leaves that fall in Méla's

wood,
And she will hear and know.

V.
THE CHILDREN LOVE ME

The children love me. Where I pass
    them by
  They overtake my way.
Caught in small hands by tunic, belt,
    and thigh,
  Of laughing need I stay.

Scarab or stone, or gathered flower,
    alike
  Their tribute-wealth they pay.
They draw me downward to the grassy
    dyke
  That lines the beaten way.

They draw me to themselves. They
    press more near
  On either hand. They lay
Their heads against my breast. Bilitis,
    dear,

They lift large eyes, and say,

Tell us of Helen. Or the Beast that came
    Huge from the ocean bed,
Of Perseus from the skies the falling
    flame,
    And of the Gorgon's head.

VI.
STILL ON THE ROUTE
THEY PASSED THE ROSES LIE

Still on the route they passed the roses
    lie:
    Still here the torches burn.
Melissa goes beneath a kinder sky
    The joy of life to learn.

Not yet for me the bridal torches glow,
    Though like of years am I.
I think her first our equal hope to know,
    And as I think, I sigh.

Shall I not also hear the nuptial song,
    The train attendant see,

The olives arched the rose-strewn path
    along,
  Some other night, for me?

For I would also break the last conceal,
  Of love at night to know;
Nor later, dearer, at my breasts to feel
  The sweet small hands forego.

VII.
*I S*ING *N*OT *L*OVES *L*ONG *C*EASED

I sing not loves long ceased, and lost
    within
  The cold receding sea.
What are the Paphian's woes, or Byblis'
    sin,
  Or Helen's arms to me?

What thirst of life was theirs, what
    hope, what fear,
  But in me beats today?
I spoil or lose, I reach or hunger here,
  And sterile shades are they.

In me, in me, the exultant pulses stir,
    As here supine I lie.
It is my life I sing. Shall life recur?
    Shall the great darkness die?

But when no more my veins their strength renew,
    When the last road I go,
Be then no cup I have not lifted too,
    No draught I did not know.

VIII.
MOTHER, SELF-BORN, FROM WHOM ALL BIRTHS MUST BE

Mother, self-born, from whom all births must be,
    Astarte of the night,
Grant me the reading of thy mystery,
    For I would serve aright.

Between thy knees the gods were born: between
    Thy breasts the daemons lay.
Thou wast and wilt be when their times

  have been,
 For thou art more than they.

Formed of thy thought herself the
  Cyprian came
 From out the bright salt sea.
Virgin thou art and spouse, and chaste
  and flame,
 For all things meet in thee.

Grant me the reading of thy mystery,
 For I would serve aright,
Mother, self-born, from whom all births
  must be,
 Astarte of the night.

IX.
THE FIRST HAD WEALTH

The first had wealth beyond a dream's
  conceit.
 A rope of pearls he gave:
A city's worth, with palace, hall, and
  street,
 Market, and ware, and slave.

The second sang my hair, a cloud that
    lay
  Night on the moving mere:
My eyes that drew him from that night
    away
  As though blue dawn were here.

The third had beauty, like a holding net
  To snare a girl's entreat.
His hands upon my naked knees he set,
  Bending to kiss my feet.

Thou hast no words to sing me (*nay,
    not me*!)
  Thou hast no pearls to pay;
Thou hast not beauty; yet I long for
    thee,
  And utter naught are they.

X.
THOU SHALT NOT SEEK ME

Thou shalt not seek me, lest thy tender
    feet

Bruise on the stony way,
But where thou art, thy present doom to meet,
My coming haste shalt stay.

Thou shalt not braid thy hair in curious wise,
Lest scorch or singe ye bear.
O Eros' victim!—loose it where it lies,
Till I shall find thee there.

Thou shalt not clothe thee, lest the cincture press
Too hard on loin or side.
Wait as thou art these hours that hourly less
Thy maiden days divide.

I would not any flaw thy pride had marred,
Nor any stain should wrong,
Save where I strain thee in embrace too hard,
Or where I kiss too long.

XI.
When the Great River to the Heights Return

When the great river to the heights return
   The snows from whence it grew,
Or when the ocean's liquid fields shall learn
   The sower's task to do.

When the great pines their rooted rocks shall cleave
   To seek the lakes below,
Or when the grass the sheltered lakes shall leave
   On the bleak heights to grow,

That morn, that only morn, the lighting sky
   Another's joys shall see.
That night another in thy place shall lie,
   Soul of my soul to me.

To me, when morning moved the
    eastern sky,
The tender words he said.
Was ever night of bliss with mine to
    vie?
Was ever dawn so red?

XII.
THE NIGHT IS DARK, IT BLINDS ME WHERE I TREAD

The night is dark, it blinds me where I
    tread;
    I cannot feel my way.
The forest climbs a tangled waste
    ahead—
Then wert thou wise to stay.

The noise of waters in the night is high:
    Loud is the fall, and near—
Thou would'st not heed him though he
    passed thee by:
His call thou would'st not hear.

The odours of the flowers of night

      prevail,
    The heavy scents oppress—
Thou would'st but swoon, that not the nightingale
    Should rouse—and he the less.

Then must I wait, with all the hills between,
    For while I dreaming lie,
He comes again to where he once hath been,
    And I can feel him nigh.

XIII.
O S*ombre* W*oods*, R*eveal* I*f* H*ere* S*he* C*ame*

O sombre woods, reveal if here she came.
    She sought the vale below.
O vale, I call again my mistress' name.
    The river trail ye know.

O river, tell me, did she wander here?
    By the great road she goes.

O road, reveal. Thy barren course is
    clear.
The city street she chose.

O happy street, that felt her naked
    tread—
She took the golden way.
O way, what closes all the space
    ahead?
The palace gates are they.

O palace, yield her whom I seek so
    far.
Beneath her breasts are bound
Pearls and great gems, for honour's
    fallen star
Herself thou hast not found.

XIV.
WHERE THE GREAT CLIFFS REPULSE THE CYPRIAN SEA

Where the great cliffs repulse the
    Cyprian sea,
On the last verge I lie.

Scarcely the first faint lights of dawn to be
    Reach the deep vault of sky.

As ere the goddess to our blinded eyes
    The wine-dark waters pearled,
So, stretched beneath, more dusk than violets, lies
    The dawn-awaiting world.

The sudden sunlight comes. Across the deep
    An instant lance it drave.
Trance-held, I watch the blinding splendour leap
    From silvered wave to wave.

I hide mine eyes. From out the shining way
    The goddess' self doth show.
There is more wonder in the dawn today
    Than mortal thought should know.

XV.
THE DAWN IS NEAR

The dawn is near. The morning rains
    descend.
  Surely I watch too long.
Drop after drop on sill and porch they
    blend,
  Falling throughout my song.

The dawn is near. The western waves
    have wet
  The stars the midnight knew.
All night I watched them drown. What
    hope is yet
  When the whole arc is through?

The young men pass. The others laugh
    to see
  But shall they gain at last,
Thais, or Glykera, or Myrtale,
  When their good days are past?

The young men pass me, and the old

>   forget.
>   Sad and most lone am I.
> But stars are mine that never wave shall
>   wet,
>   My songs, that shall not die.

XVI.
There Is No Laughter in My Heart Today

> There is no laughter in my heart today;
>   There are no tears to shed.
> Hope of delight of life is ceased away,
>   And any fear is fled.
>
> My petals fell long since in trampled
>   ways;
>   Dried is the empty stem.
> The laurels only from my part of praise
>   I have not left to them.
>
> Is this the form that Mnasidika knew,
>   That Sappho loved to sing,
> When the day's strength would every
>   night renew.
>   And every month was spring?

Implacable goddess! thy withdrawn delight
    Shall never prayer recall.
There is no laughter in my heart tonight,
    Nor any fear at all.

XVII.
I Feel Tonight the Shadow's Cold Decline

I feel tonight the shadow's cold decline.
    The noonday's heat is fled.
The darkness nears. In other skies than mine
    The feet of morning tread.

But when from life's retreat of ended days
    My body's loss ye lay,
I would not that ye weep, nor chide, nor praise
    My laureled right, but say:

She lived with Sappho on the Lesbian

shore,
Freely she loved at will,
And whom did first her fervent youth adore,
Dim-eyed, she worshipped still.

The gods who form us, and the fates who doom,
Only her end can tell.
We leave her with the roses round her tomb,
That once she loved so well.

SONGS OF BALOCHISTAN

I.
THE SONG OF THE FOOTPRINTS.

To Allah always be the praise,
For fertile plain, or rainless ways.

Though all things in their dust depart
He shall continue calm at heart.

From Hamza is our high descent:
Victory belongs the Holy Tent.

Still by the prophet's grace we are
Yäili's sons peculiar.

We came from Halab, fighting far

Through Bompür, and in Karbala.

Yazïd we fought and routed twice:
From Allah was the sacrifice.

The town of Sistän, street and store,
Dividing by the bows we bore.

At peace, while Shamsu'd-din was
    king,
We rested from our wandering.

Budru'-d-din, by evil chance,
Refused us from his countenance.

Then southward, led by Jäläl Khän,
We marched where Härïn held Makrän.

Härïn before our bowmen fled:
Through all Makrän and Këch we
    spread.

Then east and south, by gorge and fell,
We sought a surer land to dwell.

Höts in the lower plains remained:
Rinds and Lashärs the mountains
   gained.

Rinds in Shorän the streams divide:
Lashari holds Gandava-side.

A grazing-space the Dombki found
The running streams of Gäj around.

The Drishaks and Mazäris claim
The Rind support in land and name.

The Näli ground the Jistkanis
Joined with Nuhani's tribe to seize.

The Chandyas and the Kalmatis
Divided Haleb. Over these

To lead one nation, chief of all
From clouded height to water-call,

The Rind, Mïr Shaihak, ruled. Two
   score
Of thousands were the bows we bore.

This is the record of the race:
The mountains gave our resting-place.

When Chäkur ruled us, strife began
Between our nation, clan with clan.

War through the hills for thirty years
Saw kindred fall to kindred spears.

Lasharis and the Rinds were foes,
And neighbours fell to neighbours'
    bows.

This is the strife the old men tell
When Gwaharäm and Bakar fell,

Nodhbandagh of the liberal hand,
Haddë and Järo: and the band

Of Rinds red-booted, swordsmen all,
Mïr-Hän. Mïr-Hasän. first to fall

When Rinds fought backward, mile by
    mile,

The valley to the closed defile,

Till Ali and Bivaragh died,
Entrapped beneath the mountain-side.

Of Chäkur, at the last who fled,
And came years after down the head

Of Bolän pass, and smote Lashar
Through all Gandava to the far

Plain-country of the Höts. The breath
Of all things mortal ends in death.

II.
THE SONG OF SHAMBANI.

Brahim Shambänï sings. I tell
    Of Allah, God of Israel.

The torrent through my heart is deep:
Murtaza in my thought I keep.

The dust beneath His passing feet
The name of Allah doth repeat.

Who shall reveal His natal day?
What scales of earth His might shall
   weigh?

No father's steps before him trod:
He is the first and final God.

No mother at her knees hath taught:
There is no sister keeps His court.

No son behind His steps shall tread:
He dwells alone in holihed.

He hath no greed Whose hands are full:
Patient He is: the Merciful.

Five angels at His service are,
To work His wonders wide and far.

The first, Wahï, interpreteth:
The second lifts the wings of death—

He bears the name of Azräïl:

The third is Khwäja[1]: Isräïl

Is fourth—he sounds the notes that stir
All the world's winds: the trumpeter.

The last is Shaitän, proud and blind,
Who strove when Allah made mankind.

Alone before His books He sits:
No thing He adds, and naught remits.

He writeth till the page is full:
Patient He is: the Merciful.

With each man in his turn to deal
He gives the sign to Azräïl.

The angel naught will heed thereon
Of any supplication.

Of ruth his stony eyes are bare:
His heart hath neither hate nor care.

---

[1] Elijah—But he has become a river-god under this name in later Hindoo mythology!

Children he takes, and leaveth gold,
And all the wealth of flocks in fold.

He drags high princes by the hair,
From all they owned, and all they were.

These are the ways of Life and Death:
The word Brähïm Shambänï saith.

III.
THE WISDOM OF CHAKUR

The grass is green beneath the hill.
O haste, Miralis, haste and fill
Your horses' nosebags ere ye ride,
For ours is now the jungle-side.

Haibat the son of Bïbrak found
Strange camels on his grazing-ground.

To Chäkur and the Rinds he spake,
"Too loose a rule your herdsmen take."

Three times he stroked his beard and

swore,
"I will not backward bring them more.

"When next the Näri ridge they cross
Account them for a lasting loss."

* * * * * * *

The *mëhr-sirän* to Chäkur said,
"Your camels in the night are fled.

"We chased them down the mountain ways,
With Bïbrak's Näri herds they graze.

To reach their arms the tribe began,
Wide-wounding swords Egyptian,

Black-shafted spears, and matchlocks chased;
And called their feeding mares in haste.

But Chäkur spake the word that cools
Hot impulse in the hearts of fools—

"Who breaks his own right arm in ire?
Who sets his jungle grass afire?

"Ye shall not with your kinsmen strive
For all the wandered beasts alive.

"How oft the lean fakïr will claim
Such tribute in the Sacred Name."

While thus with words their wrath he
    stayed
There came a swift Lashärï raid.

The horsemen fleet of Gwaharäm,
Ere the fled herdsmen waked alarm.

Had swept and rounded, wild as wind,
The grazing camels of the Rind.

Unchecked were now the cries that
    rose,
With bridling steeds, and cording bows,

But ere the chasing horsemen showed
Blurred colour the mountain road.

Far down the pass they drave their loot,
Remote from Chäkur's urged pursuit.

The Rinds their wearied mares at length
Must halt to save their stumbling
   strength.

Chäkur with shaded eyes surveyed
Bare hills for sideward hopes of aid,

But saw no movement, near or far,
Save where the children of Lashär

Crossed with their spoil, a lengthened
   mile,
The mouth of Näri's stark defile.

Sudden a whirl of dust there came
From Näri's gorge, and fierce as flame,

With shine of brandished spears on
   high,
And scarves and turbans blown awry,

The Son of Bïbrak's troop he knew
Charge down Lashärï's thieving crew.

Relentless in their tribal hate
No thirst their slitting swords abate

Till twice a hundred lives have paid
Blood tribute for the broken raid.

Still distant from the ended war,
The Rinds the men of Haibat saw

The spoil recaptured herding back
But turned at Näri's steeper track,

Up through that sunless gorge conveyed
The booty that their swords had stayed.

More fierce than erst, the Rinds renewed
Their clamour for a neighbour-feud—

"Keep they our herds, and thine beside?"
But Chäkur yet their cries denied.

"The spoil that to our foes was lost
They rescued at a deadly cost.

"The strength on which your lives
　　depend
Ye shall not in dissension end.

"Twice lost is that Lashärï shares,
But theirs is ours, and ours is theirs.

"My curse on whom this sword shall
　　draw.
The ruling of your Mïr is law."

Days in this discord passed, until
Around that barren height of hill

The self-returning herds defiled;
Unmated fillies fleet and wild.

And playful foals that moved among
Deep-uddered dams, and big with
　　young,

And savage sires the lines that led,
Till down their native vales they spread.

Then Chäkur gave to Bïbrak's son
Free-handed meed for service done,

The huts on Näri's stream, and all
The grazing to the mountain wall.

The grass is green beneath the hill.
O haste, Miralis, haste and fill
Your horses' nosebags ere ye ride,
For ours is now the jungle-side.

IV.
THE SONG OF BIVARAGH[2]

---

[2]The Balochi attribute this song to Bivaragh, but it is more probable that it was composed by Durrak, a poet of the eighteenth century. As the Balochi have no written language, the only available evidences are those of oral tradition, and the structure of the poem, and the point is never likely to be determined with certainty.

But whoever wrote the song, the incident on which it is founded is historical. Bivaragh, a Baloch of the Rind clan, successfully abducted the daughter of the Khan of Kanda-

*The clouds on Sori's plains are low;
The thirsting desert yearns below.*

Her body sways the winds to meet;
The flowers are fragrant round her feet.

"O stranger, wash thy clothes not here:

---

har (1500 A.D.) under circumstances of exceptional audacity. He then fled for protection, not to his own clan, but to the Lashari, by which stategem he secured both sections of the Baloch nation to support his escapade.

The indignant Khan collected an army for the recovery of his daughter, and invaded Balochistan. Bivaragh was unwilling to be the cause of a sanguinary battle, and as the Khan's army approached the position occupied by the Baloch tribesmen, he offered to go out alone to reconnoitre. He succeeded in stealing his way undetected into the tent of the Khan, and then, having him at his sword's mercy, surrendered himself unconditionally! On this, the Khan became reconciled to his son-in-law, and peace was made between the opposing armies.

We learn from other legends that Bivaragh was a very prudent man.

My camels soil the water clear."

"O maid, my cloak is naught to care:
It is not as thy raiment rare."

* * * * * * *

As on black cloud the lightning glows
The sudden jewel shifts and shows.

A jewel for her throat divine;
A *häs* of silver forged and fine.

"O minstrel, come when dawn is near,
The drunken Bhäni will not hear.

"Tread softly past the sleeping khän:
Avoid the huts of Ahmad-Hän.

"This gift thy secret hand shall bear:
This song shall speak my meaning
    there—

"A day, and yet again a day:
The false world drifts like smoke away.

"A night, and yet again a night:
Recall me when the dawn is white.

"My heart is shaping to thy shape:
Thou shalt not with the noon escape.

"Dost feed in peace, thou lone
    gazelle?—
The while, upwind, I stalk thee well.

"Stretch thy swift limbs, thou racing
    mare?—
No less my weight thy back shall bear.

"For light thy petals wide are
    spread?—
The brown bee's shade is overhead."

* * * * * * *

The moons grow larger night by night.
Hast learnt the dangered paths aright?

The fourteenth moon is overhead—

The brown bee in thy cup doth tread.

The lands of Sori, plain and plain,
Are dark with cloud and drifting rain.

V.
SHIRËN

What prince to loose her girdle claims?
Shirën is still the name of names.

The old king asked, "In lands afar
What princes as my daughter are?"

They told, "There is no prince is meet
To hold her velvet-sandalled feet.

"What hand the restless zebra tames?
Shirën is still the name of names."

A stone a hundred *maunds* in weight
Was rolled beside the temple gate.

"Who would Shirën, my daughter, wed
Must grind this stone to dust," he said.

* * * * * * *

The madman backward bound his hair:
He stripped his arm and shoulder bare.

Alone within her tent she prayed,
"Allah, my lover's smiting aid."

A year with ceaseless toil he smote:—
The dust is in his parching throat:

The stone dissolves beneath his blows:
As black surmä the powder flows.

* * * * * * *

The old king spake, "This churl to slay
I will not tale the price I pay.

"Red gold I will not count nor weigh
To whom shall steal his life away."

"For gold unweighed," the beldam said,
"Is none that lives who were not dead."

With words of craft she sought Parät—
"I greet thee with a grieving heart.

"In Alläh's book the maiden read:
The grave became her bridal bed."

* * * * * * *

Beneath the wall the bearers trod.
She asked, "Who goeth forth to God?"

"Tis young Parät," the bearers said,
"Who swifter than the dawn was dead."

"O nurse," she said, "the child ye nurst
Is for her lover's arms athirst;

"And you must rise and braid my hair,
And the red *chädär* I will wear."

"No prince was young Parät," she said,
"You would not weep a craftsman
      dead?"

"O Daï, foolish words we speak;
I was not made to princes meek."

In Alläh's book the maiden read:
The grave became her bridal bed.

He in that other world than this
Her velvet-sandalled feet shall kiss.

No prince to loose her girdle claims:
Shirën is still the name of names.

VI.
THE MARRIAGE-SONG OF DURRAK[3]

While dawn intends along the darkened
    sky,
  The praise to God I bring.
O friends, regard the lofty strain I try!

---

[3] Jam Darrak was a Baluch poet, who lived in the eighteenth century. Tradition says that he fell in love with a girl attached to the zenana of the Khan of Kalät, and remained at his court in consequence, where he was subjected to many persecutions before he obtained the lady.

O minstrels, touch my string!

O minstrels, sing it where the princes
    sit!
The strings of golden gut
Shall find no song for royal mirth more
    fit
Till the last chord is cut.

I met her singly in the thronged bazaar,
    In Dhädar's market-place.
Only I knew in all that wealthed *darbär*
    The temple of her face.[4]

I said, "A year of service-troth I pay.
    My palace-haunt is here."
Were all the undreamed delights an
    only day?
    Or all the days a year?

Three paroquets in my love's garden
    are.

---

[4] It was not the custom of the women of Baluchistan to walk veiled at the period to which this poem belongs.

No fairer joys afford
The triple flowers like sistered pearls
    that star
    The garden of my Lord.

What braided crown as regal lifts as
    here?
    What other lips as red?
Pomegranates part a mouth as vermeil-
    dear
    Ere the full flower is spread.

Now face to face we take our final gain.
    Abundant beauties yield
Bright swords by which my former
    griefs are slain:
    Showers for a starving field.

Life makes unloth its last surrender
    now,
    Raptured, and held, and whole...
Jamäl and Zëwä[5] hear my bridal vow
    That evil leaves my soul.

---

[5] Peris who watch over the welfare of devout brides.

www.ingramcontent.com/pod-product-compliance
Lightning Source LLC
Chambersburg PA
CBHW032021040426
42448CB00006B/694